ORIGINAL LYRIC COMPOSITION

A song of love, wisdom, and Christianity

ERWIN PARENT

Prominent Books

Dedicated to my two wonderful wives,
Virginia Allen Parent
and
Rosanna Gibson Parent

CONTENTS

INTRODUCTION

Music has always been an important part of my life. When I was a child, my father used to listen to classical music on the radio, also he had some vinyl records he use to play.

Frequently. My mother would take us on Saturdays to Arthur Fiedler's Children Concert at the Esplanade along the Charles River in Boston.

My first wife, Virginia had a beautiful Mezzo Soprano voice and frequently sang solos in our church. Living in Boston's Back Bay area, we also belonged to the Boston Opera group and attended at Faneuil Hall.

I always loved to hear duets. The separate male and female voices and then a combined duet. To me, this was very moving and inspiring.

The Music contained in this book, was my struggle to write lyrics, hoping that someday it could be put to music. I entered several Lyric-Writing contests and always got good reviews but could never find anyone to help me accomplish my goal.

Gospel

I expect these may be sung in churches.
Whether by a choir or individual soloists.

THE HOMELESS

In God's kingdom, there are none homeless
Only those who are troubled or afraid
Jesus saw them dwell among the tombs
Farmers left them food giving them aid

    If you're homeless listen to the music,
    It's hanging in the air everywhere
    All those hymns sung for centuries
    Sing along with them lift your voices high
    The words will nourish you don't be shy
    Listen to the music it's hanging in the air
    Words will become an answered prayer

Sense that inner feeling pulling you aside
Trying to make right years gone wrong
Feel the hug from God showing you are loved
All mankind wants you where you belong

    If you're homeless listen to the music,
    It's hanging in the air everywhere
    All those hymns sung for centuries
    Sing along find that inner peace
    The words will nourish you don't be shy
    Listen to the music it's hanging in the air
    Words will become an answered prayer

LADDER TO HEAVEN

Life seems an endless struggle with problems every day
We can reach out to God and pray that we find a way
Let's climb the ladder to heaven the one that Jacob dreamed
Many have climbed it before and have been fully redeemed

       I'm on the ladder to heaven I can hear the Angels singing
       In heavenly celebrations listen to those church bells ringing
       My precious list is long of those I hope to see
       A happy reunion oh what a happy reunion there will be

As we climb, each rung gets easier the happier we become
We climb with steady progress with the beating of a drum
Upward we climb happily now finally being delivered
No looking back and no regrets as we are liberated

       I'm on the ladder to heaven the Gates of Pearl is insight
       I've come from the pit of darkness into a heavenly light
       My precious list is long of those I plan to see
       A happy reunion oh what a happy reunion there will be.

I WILL WORK WITH GOD

I will listen to the desperate needs of others
Help me hear the voice of them in need
The Master showed us how this was done,
I will work with God to help them as they plead.

I will look for those many who seek blessings,
Help me see even those hidden where they are
The Master helped so many out of sight,
I will work with God to see them near and far.

> I will work with God He is listening to me,
> Bring on those many with desperate needs,
> Gather those who hunger so He can feed,
> Collect all those who seek His blessings,
> Get those who are in need of healings,
> I am working with God He is listening to me.

I will always try to be in my right place
Help me choose the right path to take
The Master headed in the right direction,
I will work with God for that choice to make.

I will reach out to heal by touch or by thought,
Help me with the healing and prayers I need
The Master reached out and healed many this way,
I will pray to God to perform this simple deed.

> I will work with God He is listening to me,
> Bring on those many with desperate needs,
> Gather those who hunger so He can feed,
> Collect all those who seek His blessings,
> Get those who are in need of healings,
> I am working with God He is listening to me.

IF JESUS HAD A CELLPHONE

If Jesus had a Cellphone, would he call you or me
What pictures would he download for us to see
Would he send a text with words of happiness
Would he send directions to those we need to bless

    Oh, Jesus call on me, send a text for me to see
    Let this be my daily bread I know you are there for me
    We will listen for thy voice lest we go astray
    Oh, Master call on me let me help in some way
    A faithful follower you can always count on me
    Your message I will share you can count on me

If Jesus had a Cellphone, would he call you or me
Would he ask us to report on who we have set free
If he asked to see results what would we say
What if he asked who we helped today

    Oh, Jesus call on me send a text for me to see
    Let this be my daily bread I know your there for me
    We will listen for thy voice lest we go astray
    Oh Master call on me let me help in some way
    A faithful follower you can always count on me
    Your message I will share you can count on me

WE IMAGINE

Some stars we see tonight may not be there,
They may have vanished eons and eons ago
Yet this reflected light has shown to mariners
And wanderers for centuries the way to go

> Imagine. This former presence is still
> Blessing and shining in heavens height,
> Still guides the mariner and astronaut
> And still beautifies the darkest night.

Some of earth's greatest men and women
Have long-vanished ages and ages ago
Yet their goodness has blessed us and given
Inspiration and hope to many who are low.

> Imagine. Do we not admire the devotion of Ruth?
> And Esther; feels the love of the Messiah
> Marvel at the faith of Daniel and David,
> Cherish the trust of Moses and Noah?

Our loved ones, precious in our lives,
May have long vanished from our view
Yet their qualities are still with us,
And continue in memories, not a few.

> Imagine. Their light still brightly shines
> Can we not feel their warmth and tenderness?
> Sense the strength of their presence, cherish how
> They blessed our lives with joy and happiness.

RESTORATION

We lament over many things that in time were lost,
Material things accumulated each with dearest cost
And many things we feel that cannot be replaced,
Lie like broken promises in heaps of utter waste.
We anguish over many dreams that yet lie unfilled,
Or over the enthusiasm we one day even killed

    We can hear the answer, but we need to listen,
    We can run the race but we need to hasten
    We can speak God's word when we are silent,
    We can see God's Truth when we repent.
    We have Gods' promises that still cannot be beaten,
    Restoring all the years that the locusts hath eaten.

If we could only live again some of those many days,
What would we correct to make them happy ways?
We cannot take back all the words unwisely spoken,
Or mend many promises that since have been broken
But we do have the time to piece all things together,
We do have the faith that all things we can weather.

    We can hear the answer, but we need to listen,
    We can run the race but we need to hasten
    We can speak God's word when we are silent,
    We can see God's Truth when we repent.
    We have Gods' promises that still cannot be beaten,
    Restoring all the years that the locusts hath eaten.

THE DARKNESS AND THE LIGHT

Creator of the earth, the Sun and Moon,
Your goodness is the same midnight or noon
As frightened children fleeing from the night,
We race into the safety of the light
We need not fear when shadows start to fall
Or think that on your help we cannot call
Or think in the morning things will be alright,
Perfection is eternal day or night.

> Lord, we need not fret nor to thy shelter flee,
> The darkness and the light are both alike to thee.
> The fullest Moon will never harm the tree,
> Lazarus was awakened and set free,
> While in your presence, shadows flee
> The darkness and the light are both alike to thee.

We need not fear that death is master here,
Or feel the loss of someone held so dear
The dream is no more real, day or night,
Illusions are not real but based on sight
If we dwell in deepest pits of despair,
As Daniel thrown into the Lion's Lair
The Father's way is always best and bright,
The Ark was safe not only day but night.

> Lord, we need not fret nor to thy shelter flee,
> The darkness and the light are both alike to thee.
> The fullest Moon will never harm the tree,
> Lazarus was awakened and set free,
> While in your presence, shadows flee
> The darkness and the light are both alike to thee.

Love

Love. How can we live without it?
What would life be like without it?
When it's lost, how do we find love
again? How long should we wait?

"Love never fails. (I Corinthians 13:8)

I THANK GOD FOR YOU

You came into my life one day and I've never been the same,
You gave me hope once again and set my heart aflame
You lifted spirits bending low you made me smile once more,
You gave me tender constant care you made my senses soar.

You came into my mind one day and I've never been the same,
You gave me balance once again like pictures in a frame
You added color to my sight which saw only black and white,
You lit a candle in the dark and took away the night.

> Thank God, thank God for you
> I can't believe the dream came true,
> I never thought I would find you
> Thank God, thank God for you.

You came into my heart one day and I've never been the same,
You rekindled love again and fanned its dying flame
You welcomed me into your life like fingers in a glove,
You mended my broken heart and strengthened it with love.

You came into my soul one day and I've never been the same,
You gave me joy when none, you made my anguish tame
You filled my emptiness with happiness once more,
You took away the pain one day and filled my treasure store.

> Thank God, thank God for you
> I can't believe the dream came true,
> I never thought I would find you
> Thank God, thank God for you.

SECRETS SHARED

Why do I stare at her in utter fascination?
How does she captivate my total concentration?
Is it because of her million-dollar smile?
Or is it the charming way in which she beguiles?
Is it contained in the thinking that we dared?
Or is it hidden in the secrets that we shared?

Why do I share with her my innermost thoughts?
Why when we touch is my stomach all in knots?
Why do I still hear the music that she sang?
What is it that makes me on her every word hang?
Is it contained in the ways in which we cared?
Or is it hidden in the secrets that we shared?

> Secrets need a safe place only two will know
> Secrets can be hidden in the back of the mind,
> Secrets should be the hardest thing to find.
> Secrets, secrets count on me I will find a place,
> Only we will know when we are face to face,
> Secrets need a safe place only two will know.

How she can be sometimes like a helpless child,
And then in the next completely free and wild?
Why do I feel like I'm floundering in the sea?
How does make all my many troubles flee?
Is it contained in the thinking that we dared?
Or is it hidden in the secrets that we shared?

Why do I find her in the hallways of my mind?
Or still, smell perfume long after we have dined?
I remember well the sweetness of our first kiss,
Why am I afraid that something may go amiss?
Is it contained in the souls which we bared?
Or is it hidden in the secrets that we shared?

Secrets need a safe place only two will know
Secrets can be hidden in the back of the mind,
Secrets should be the hardest thing to find.
Secrets, secrets count on me I will find a place,
Only we will know when we are face to face,
Secrets need a safe place only two will know.

MAGIC OF THE CANDLE

I want the magic of the candle to dwell within my home,
To scare away the demons wherever they may roam
It will shine in darkened corners and other hidden places,
It will expose the scary and often frightening faces.

I want the magic of the candle to dwell where we dine
I want to see light filtered through my glass of wine
I want to see the candlelight dancing in your eyes,
I want to hear your happiness in a million sighs.

    Magic Candle dwell with me,
    Help me see the shadows flee
    Shine your light everywhere,
    Help us find a love so rare,
    Magic Candle dwell with me,
    Help me see the shadows flee
    Shine your light everywhere,
    Help us find the love to share.

There is no history here – no need to bring the past,
The candle will ensure us that love alone will last
We will always bask in the healing of the light,
The magic of the candle will help us through the night.

I want the magic of the candle to dwell where I abide,
I always want to know that you are at my side
I want to see our shadows reflected from the light,
Listening to the music we will dance away the night.

Magic Candle dwell with me,
Help me see the shadows flee
Shine your light everywhere,
Help us find a love so rare,
Magic Candle dwell with me,
Help me see the shadows flee
Shine your light everywhere,
Help us find the love to share.

I LOVE YOU MORE

I love you more than words can possibly express,
More than all the stars in heaven we could guess
I love you more than there are mountains here to climb,
More than all the clocks that measure endless time
I love you more each time you speak my name,
Or hear your voice, now even music's not the same
I Love you more each time I look into your eyes,
I see into the very depths of where love lies
I love you more each time I feel your touch,
Just to hold your hand, to me, means so much.

      I love you more than I could ever imagine
      Tell me that you love me one more time,
      Let it echo in the hallways of my mind
      It will be there tucked away when needed,
      It will be there in a place that I can find.

I love you more each time I smell your hair,
It fills my senses something beyond compare
I love you more each time we kiss good night,
You take away my breath, darkness becomes light
I love you more than heaven's garment hem can reach
More than all the grains of sand upon the beach
I love you more each passing day when you are near,
The hours seem like weeks when you're not here
I love you more than I could possibly confess,
I do not think that I could ever love you less.

      I love you more than I could ever imagine
      Let me see love in your eyes one more time,
      Let me look into the very depths of your soul
      I can see that you and I will never be apart,
      It means for us both that together we are whole.

THE NIGHT YOU LEFT ME

I was with you that terrible night you died
I held your hand did you sense I was near
Slipping away, I prayed that you would stay
I told you I loved you hoping you could hear

    The night you left me,
    You were growing those angel wings
    You were slipping away, I said don't go
    I could hear that song the angels sing
    You were slipping away, I said don't go
    They are waiting for you at the Gates of Pearl
    You are so incredible, I sensed you were chosen

We were alone in that final moment you and I
I know we will meet again in a much better place
I would not want to say goodbye any other way
I cherish the time we had and look to that embrace

    The night you left me,
    I saw you climb that ivory stairway to heaven
    Don't turn around I said, hoping that you would
    They are waiting for you at the Gates of Pearl
    You are so incredible, I sensed you were chosen
    Don't turn around I said, hoping that you would
    They are waiting for you at the Gates of Pearl

LIFE WITHOUT YOU

Your lovely smile no longer greets my day
Nor your laughter, lifting my spirits anew
Your presence no longer lights up the room
Such now is my life without you

> My life without you needs a bouquet,
> No need for me to find words to say
> Each flower has meaning of its own
> Each flower loved where it was grown
> This will express my love for you
> I will bring you bouquets, not a few

How can life be described, except lifeless
Like going through motions without purpose
You were the reason for my existence
You were my right arm, I'm now armless

> My life without you needs a bouquet,
> This is a reminder that I'm still near
> I will gather flowers where they grow
> Find them on hillsides where they glow
> I will bring you bouquets every day
> And place them gently where you lay

THERE IS A RIVER

Life is not the same since you passed away,
The Moon has lost its special glow
The flowers don't smell quite as sweet,
The nights are not like I used to know.

There is a river shining bright,
I saw it in a dream one night
I saw you standing on the shore,
You looked as beautiful as before
Someday soon I shall return,
We'll walk again in the moonlight
By that river, I dreamed one night,
By that river shining bright.

Now the Moon has a special glow,
I now awake to greet the dawn
The flowers have a fragrance sweet,
I feel like I've been re-born.

There is a river shining bright,
I saw it in a dream one night
I saw you standing on the shore,
You looked as beautiful as before
Someday soon I shall return,
We'll walk again in the moonlight
By that river, I dreamed one night,
By that river shining bright.

ONE MORE TIME

Tell me that you love me one more time,
Let it echo in the hallways of my mind
It will be there tucked away when needed,
It will be there in a place that I can find.

Let me smell your hair one more time,
The essence fills the chambers of my mind
Let it calm the waters of a troubled soul,
It will be there should I be left behind.

> Tell me that you love me one more time,
> You electrify my soul with each touch,
> Let me see love in your eyes one more time,
> Everything thing you do means so much.

Reach out and touch me one more time,
Let the feeling caress my soul evermore
It will electrify my senses like nothing else
It will sooth my yearning to the very core.

Let me see love in your eyes one more time,
Let me look into the very depths of your soul
I can see that you and I will never be apart,
It will mean once again that we are whole.

> Tell me that you love me one more time,
> You electrify my soul with each touch,
> Let me see love in your eyes one more time,
> Everything thing you do means so much.

BEYOND THE VEIL NOW

You're somewhere beyond the veil now,
Still thinking, dreaming, and wishing
Just as before. I'm on this side,
Thinking, dreaming, and missing.

You're somewhere in another place now,
Still organizing, planning, decorating
Just as before. I'm on this side,
Seeing the things you did, benefiting

> You're beyond the veil, I can hear your voice
> Can you sing for me our favorite hymn?
> I will sing on this side our heavenly duet
> We can meet here each night with Him

You're somewhere beyond view now,
Still smiling, laughing, and loving
Just as before. I'm on this side,
Remembering, coping, and aching.

You're somewhere beyond the veil now,
Still being your usual lovely self
Just as before. I'm on this side,
Trying my best to be my usual self.

> You're beyond the veil, I can hear your voice
> Can you tell me that you still love me?
> I will be here saying the same to you
> One day I will be there with you to see.

MY WEDDING RING

It circles my heart and makes me complete,
I cherish those happy times it brought to me
How proud I was to be your spouse,
I think that I will wear it for eternity.

It is endless, as memories, I have of you,
Some have faded but are still there
You placed it on my finger long ago,
To remove it now – a thought I cannot bear.

> Golden ring on your finger is on my mind
> I can still hear the pastor's wedding vows
> I remember looking into your beautiful eyes
> I still remember the wedding kiss even now
> All this like you will be in my mind forever
> My wedding ring remains on my finger forever.

It is as solid and complete as our marriage
The ups and downs we shared with courage
It was a magnificent brave adventure,
Thank you for sharing this happy voyage.
It is unbroken like our vows,
The words we wrote and taken deeply
Words uttered cannot be taken back,
I think that I will wear it for eternity.

> Golden ring on your finger is on my mind
> I can still hear the pastor's wedding vows
> I remember looking into your beautiful eyes
> I still remember the wedding kiss even now
> All this like you will be in my mind forever
> My wedding ring remains on my finger forever

GABRIELLE

As the father of three sons, I wonder,
What have I missed without a daughter?
Your name was chosen it seems so sad,
Gabrielle, you are the daughter I never had.

Here you are on my mind when I am old,
The new-born I never had a chance to hold
There will always be a place in my heart,
You know that we will never be apart.

> Gabrielle, you are the daughter I never had,
> Think what we missed it seems so sad
> The nursery floor un-walked, songs unsung,
> To hear you loudly test your lungs.

Perhaps we will meet in another time,
I'll polish up my nursery rhymes
Perhaps we will meet in another place,
When I can look into your lovely face.

I will always keep you right on my mind,
I'll keep looking until I'm able to find
Gabrielle your brothers will welcome you,
We will keep looking then out of the blue

> Gabrielle, you are the daughter I never had,
> Think what we missed – it seems so sad
> The wedding aisle yet un-walked,
> The conversations yet un-talked.

(Authors note – I was 76 before my first Granddaughter was born. After moving in with my son and his family a few years later, a second granddaughter was born, named Aubree. I loved holding her. One night she was in my arms when she fell asleep. I carried her upstairs to her crib and laid her down. I stood there and sobbed, saying Gabrielle it is another time)

Patriotic

Being in the military is an honor; to serve your country is special. I was fortunate not to face combat.

My hat is off to those who had this experience, some more than once.

When WWII broke out, I was 7 years old. But I remember the blackouts and the air raid warnings. I was listening to the radio when the report came in that Pearl Harbor had been bombed.

THE WHITE CROSSES

The bravest of the brave who stormed the beach at Normandy,
Now lie in rows of endless crosses as far as eye can see
Their hopes and dreams are shattered and lie unfulfilled,
The families left at home whose futures have been stilled.

    For those laying beneath the row of white crosses,
    They are listening to the beat of a different drummer,
    They are marching side by side in an infinite number
    No rank nor race nor gender separates them now,
    We will never fight again the weary world will vow
    Where is the peace? Where has that promise gone, we ask?
    It held such promise, it seemed like such a simple task,
    It must come from within each heart to end all warfare,
    It is the task of humankind it is our own cross to bear.

The bravest of the brave, who stormed the beach at Normandy,
Now lie in rows of endless crosses as far as eye can see
Their hopes and dreams buried there where they lay,
Their families never had a homecoming day.

    For those laying beneath the row of white crosses,
    They are listening to the beat of a different drummer,
    They are marching side by side in an infinite number
    No rank nor race nor gender separates them now,
    We will never fight again the weary world will vow
    Where is the peace? Where has that promise gone, we ask?
    It held such promise, it seemed like such a simple task,
    It must come from within each heart to end all warfare,
    It is the task of humankind it is our own cross to bear.

GLIDING TO HEAVEN

Gliders on the left and right fill the morning sky,
God will guide us all the way leading like a dove
The wind beneath our wings guides us to the ground,
We have purpose and faith thanks to God above.

As we circle towards the ground we will pray,
That we can land safely and begin our mission
God will guide us to the place we need to be,
We will meet with others sustaining the vision.

> Gliding, gliding we are going to Heaven
> Listen, listen to those church bells ringing,
> I can even hear those angels singing,
> I will look for you at the Gates of Pearl,
> Gliding, gliding we are going to Heaven.

Gliders on the left and gliders on the right,
Circling in the sky greeting the dawn
Closing the circle as we move to the ground,
Looking for the safest spot like a giant swan.

Training for months gives us a special bond,
Devoted to the cause a special group of men
Relying on each other with an unending trust,
Some of us later may be gliding to heaven.

> Gliding, gliding we are going to Heaven
> Listen, listen to those church bells ringing,
> I can even hear those angels singing,
> I will look for you at the Gates of Pearl,
> Gliding, gliding we are going to Heaven.

PLACING FLOWERS AT MY HEADSTONE

When placing flowers at my headstone,
I request they be red, white and blue
I want to first honor our flag,
And then all that we hold so true.

One a Blue Bell and give me not a few,
It's a reminder to never hang our head
Keep our head held high and be proud
Like many of my brothers here dead.

> Placing flowers at my headstone,
> If you do these simple things for me,
> You will my faith and honor renew
> My eyes will be focused on heaven,
> At attention, I'll be saluting you.

White Carnations for innocence lost,
A reminder of a life unfulfilled
All the things that could have been,
Like our farmland lying untilled.

Bright red Roses for lives unlived,
Of our families never seen again
A wife and children we never had,
Like the fate of an abandoned train.

> Placing flowers at my headstone,
> If you do these simple things for me,
> You will my faith and honor renew
> My eyes will be focused on heaven,
> At attention, I'll be saluting you.

MY AMERICAN FLAG

It's been raised in many places,
It's been damaged in the fight
It may be tattered and torn,
But it's there in morning light.

It's been raised in highest places,
It's what our enemies hate to see
But to it our soldier's rally,
And from it, our enemies flee.

Wave on my American Flag,
Wave on your flag of beauty,
Our stars and stripes live on
They can see you from home,
They can see you from heaven.

If burned or stomped on,
It's still flying in our mind
For every flag burned or lost,
Three more will we find.

So, treat it with some respect,
It's not just a plain old rag
So many Americans have died,
Hold high my American flag.

Wave on my American flag,
Wave on you flag of beauty,
Our stars and stripes live on
They can see you from home,
They can see you from heaven.

UKRAINE YOU REIGN

Ukraine you are the leading star of the world,
We are all watching and hoping you get aid
We never thought this evil can happen again
We watch as you are brave and never afraid.

    Ukraine, Ukraine you reign, you reign
    Your people stay some flee to safety
    The world must vow never again
    God help save Kyiv our mother city

Putin must be condemned and charged,
Bucha must never happen again, enough
Take note evil North Korea and China,
The world is saying enough, enough

    Ukraine, Ukraine you reign, you reign
    Zelenskyy the brave will never flee
    He is a World Leader without a doubt
    Ukraine will rebuild and be set free.